Surviving
The Storms
of Stress

Discovery Series Bible Study

Ron Hutchcraft is a popular author, speaker, seminar leader, and radio host. I've known him to be an enthusiastic and tireless servant of the Lord—well, almost tireless. A few years ago, Ron wrote a book relating how the stress of his busy schedule and endless family responsibilities almost did him in. He learned some valuable lessons about dealing with modern stress, and he has shared these lessons in his book *Living Peacefully In A Stressful World*, available from Discovery House Publishers.

This booklet is the "wrap-up chapter" of Ron's book. I think you'll find his insights not only creative and practical but also drawn from the unending well of heaven's wisdom.

Martin R. De Haan II, President of RBC Ministries

Publisher: Discovery House Publishers
Managing Editor: Bill Crowder
Editor: Anne Cetas
Graphic Design: Alex Soh, Ineke
Cover Photo: Alex Soh © 2005 RBC Ministries Asia Ltd.
Study Guide: Bill Crowder, Sim Kay Tee

This *Discovery Series Bible Study* is based on "Surviving The Storms Of Stress" (HP011), one of the popular *Discovery Series* booklets from RBC Ministries. With more than 140 titles on a variety of biblical and Christian-living issues, these 32-page booklets offer a rich resource of insight for your study of God's Word.

For a catalog of *Discovery Series* booklets, write to us at:
RBC Ministries, PO Box 2222, Grand Rapids, MI 49555-2222
Or, visit us on the Web at: www.discoveryseries.org

This study guide is based on a portion of the book *Living Peacefully In A Stressful World* by Ron Hutchcraft. Ron is a popular author, speaker, and seminar leader, and hosts the daily national radio program *A Word With You.*

Living Peacefully In A Stressful World is published by Discovery House Publishers, a member of the RBC family of ministries. For more information about Discovery House or for a list of their biblical resources, visit their Web site at www.dhp.org. You can also contact DHP by calling 1-800-653-8333 or writing to:
Discovery House Publishers
P. O. Box 3566
Grand Rapids, MI 49501-3566

A member of the RBC Ministries family:
Our Daily Bread, Day Of Discovery, RBC Radio, Discovery Series,
Our Journey, Loving God Series, Discovery House Music

ISBN 1-57293-183-3

Table Of Contents

Our
Enslaving
Expectations

Commercials play to our restlessness, and they even help to create it. If they succeed, we feel a need for their product by the time their pitch is over. We want better breath, smoother hands, a nicer smell, or a bigger burger.

One classic potato chip commercial shows a boy boarding a bus with a big bag of their crunchies. As the boy keeps reaching for another chip, he claims, "Bet you can't eat just one." Hearing the irresistible crunch, the bus driver grabs "just one." Of course, he keeps munching, until finally his hat is full of those habit-forming chips. By the end of the ad, everyone on the bus is chomping and singing, "No one can eat just one." That's amazing, when you consider that you can't even get two people to speak to each other on the buses I ride!

But the advertisers are experts on human motivation. They want to create in us the appetite for more. Even without those commercials, we are driven by that appetite.

"More" is usually perceived as the answer to our restlessness, the "if-only-I-had's" of life. We convince ourselves that there's nothing wrong with us that wouldn't be cured by more time, more house, more money, more friends, more job, more clothes, more excitement, more comforts.

Then we get the "two aspirin" form of a big raise, a dream home, a partner, a lighter schedule, or a standing ovation—only to find that the "headache" of restlessness soon returns.

The unsettling truth is that more is never enough! Discontentment destroys any possibility of personal peace. It condemns us to the pressure cooker of guaranteed restlessness.

Advertisers are experts in human motivation. They want to create in us an appetite for more.

Conventional wisdom tells us, "A man's reach should always exceed his grasp." A commitment to excellence, to service, to personal purity should keep us reaching. We are, by nature, pursuers. That's why God calls us to pursue peace! But much modern stress results from the wrong pursuits—misplaced discontentment.

We are enslaved by expectations that cannot be satisfied. They are intrinsically frustrating. These "drivers" come in three forms, and they keep us on edge because they keep us reaching for more.

1. Possession Expectations

Plato commented insightfully on our possession expectations:

> Poverty consists not in the decrease of one's possession but in the increase of one's greed.

There is always another "thing" you don't have! And the increase of things only creates an appetite for more. There was a time we looked forward to owning one TV, but then we needed two. Once we were thrilled with an apartment of our own, but the thrill was soon replaced with a hankering for a little house of our own. Eventually the little house was too little. It would take a big house to do the trick. And a swimming pool would be nice too.

Our "poverty" really is, in Plato's words, "the increase of one's greed." Dinner out at McDonald's was a once-special treat—now it's routine. Tonight it will take a fancy restaurant to provide the same special treat. It seems only yesterday that an air conditioner was the luxury of the rich—today I've got to have one. Yesterday's luxury has become today's necessity.

Life's goodies are truly good when God provides them in His way and in His time. They are enslaving when we demand them—when we expect them. Possession expectations will keep pushing us past the fragile limits of peace.

2. People Expectations

We live in a state of chronic frustration because the significant others in our lives don't measure up. Or can't measure up.

Author James Dobson points out that while the baby is on the way, we profess only to want a child who is normal. But from birth on, we want a superkid! We want for him either the life we didn't have or a replay of the life we did have. Somehow, their grades, their friends, their style are never good enough. We focus on what they need to improve, seldom on what they have achieved.

> **We live in a state of chronic frustration because the significant others in our lives don't measure up.**

So our children are quickly caught up with us in the whirlpool of more.

Marriages become battlefields because our partners continually disappoint us. Weaknesses are magnified; strengths are forgotten—just the reverse of the courtship process. We are expecting more of Prince Charming or Cinderella, and they may be getting tired of never being enough.

These people expectations can make a person incurably restless with his work. No working conditions, no boss is what you really want. And the dissatisfaction syndrome can reach right into the church too. There is ultimately something wrong with every pastor, every leader. We end up expecting of people around us a perfection that belongs only to God.

If you are not satisfied with those around you, you are probably even less satisfied with yourself. We compare ourselves to standards of parenting, partnering, or producing that are unattainable, and can never relax because we are never good enough.

Marsha grabbed me after church one day to pour out her broken heart over her prodigal son. She had tried so hard and done everything she could, and he was walking on the wild side of life. As we talked, it became evident that Marsha had an unreasonably high standard for her son, one he could never quite hit. I suggested to her that a child who is never good enough may one day stop trying to be. He may choose a rebellious course that will remove any possibility of impossible expectations. Her son had opted out of the demands, only to create a whole new arena of pressure.

> **If our hopes for peace are placed in the hands of imperfect people, they are bound to evaporate.**

Marsha began to cry as she revealed the reason she had pushed her son so hard. She had grown up in the brokenness left by an alcoholic father. Her youthful agony made her resolve to be a perfect mother and to have a perfect home. She had walked that tightrope for years, and her son's struggles always threatened her goals. If he wasn't good enough, then she wasn't good enough. She was always reaching for more from him, and from herself. Neither of them could find peace.

If our hopes for peace are placed in the hands of imperfect people, they are bound to evaporate.

3. Performance Expectations

Performance drives us to stressful schedules, sacrifices, and compromises. Our worth becomes identified with our work, and no spot on the mountain is enough. Even the top is unsatisfying, as Alexander the Great discovered when he wept because there were no more worlds to conquer.

Amy started high school with the futility of performance expectations. She seemed sad most of the time, so sad that she found herself on the brink of suicide. Although she outgrew those depths of depression, she did not grow much of a smile. The irony of her personal dissatisfaction was that she was a high achiever! She was elected vice president of her school chorus, but she was miserable because she was not president. She ranked second in her class academically, but she chose to look at the one student ahead of her rather than the 300 behind her. The storm in Amy seldom abated because winning was her only option.

Whatever our game is, we will lose consistently if we have to win. We aspire to be promoted to the next rung on the company ladder—only to need yet the next promotion before the paint is dry on our new office door. No award, no achievement is ever enough. We punish our bodies, our families, our friends, our sanity to reach for another level of victory.

One day this unquenchable appetite for conquest can even violate the marriage covenant. There is the "need" to demonstrate that you are still attractive. The innocent flirtations are tantalizing. You, your spouse, your kids—and even your conquest—end up sacrificed on the ugly altar of adultery.

Discontentment is the mortal enemy of peace— a deep root of stress and restlessness.

It is stress-driven slavery to always have something to prove. Discontentment runs like a treadmill under our feet. We are always running, pushing for more possessions, more from people, more conquest. There is no rest on a treadmill. Discontentment is the mortal enemy of peace—a deep root of stress and restlessness.

Instead, consider the apostle Paul's equation for contentment:

Godliness with contentment is great gain. For we brought nothing into the world, and we can take nothing out of it. But if we have food and clothing, we will be content with that (1 Tim. 6:6-8).

STUDY NO. **1**

Creating Stress

1 Timothy 6:6—"Now godliness with contentment is great gain."

Objective:
To recognize how we create unnecessary stress in our lives.

Bible Memorization:
1 Timothy 6:6

Read:
"Our Enslaving Expectations"
pp.5-9

Warming Up

On a scale of 0 to10, how would you grade your "stress level" at this point of your life? What would you identify as the main source(s) of your stress?

Thinking Through

Do you agree that advertisements (p.5) are a major cause of stress? Why? How have commercials created discontentment and, as a result, stress in your life?

How accurate is Plato when he says, "Poverty consists not in the decrease of one's possession but in the increase of one's greed"? (p.6).

In what ways (p.8) can our worth be identified with our work or our performance, instead of being identified by our character?

Digging In
Key Text: 1 Timothy 6:6-10

In v.6, we see the elements of true spiritual "gain"— godliness and contentment. What do these ideas describe, and how do they work together for our gain?

What dangers (v.9) await those who pursue riches as their life's goal? What could be the end result of those dangerous priorities?

Is it a sin to want to be rich? Why or why not? In Paul's warning, what danger is connected with wanting to be rich? What outcome awaits those who ignore these warnings?

Going Further
Refer
In Hebrews 13:5-6, we see grounds for true personal and spiritual contentment. What are those things? Why are they different from wealth and what it can buy?

Reflect
Of the three kinds of expectations highlighted in this session, which one gives you the most stress and adversely impacts your life? Specifically, are you satisfied with your salary? Your house? Your car? Your spouse? Your children? Your current situation in life? Why? Why not?

Review 1 Timothy 6:6-10 once again. How can you tell whether you are loving money or God the most?

"⁶Now godliness with contentment is great gain. ⁷For we brought nothing into this world, and it is certain we can carry nothing out. ⁸And having food and clothing, with these we shall be content. ⁹But those who desire to be rich fall into temptation and a snare, and into many foolish and harmful lusts which drown men in destruction and perdition. ¹⁰For the love of money is a root of all kinds of evil, for which some have strayed from the faith in their greediness, and pierced themselves through with many sorrows."
1 Timothy 6:6-10

"⁵Let your conduct be without covetousness; be content with such things as you have. For He Himself has said, 'I will never leave you nor forsake you.' ⁶So we may boldly say: 'The Lord is my helper; I will not fear. What can man do to me?' "
Hebrews 13:5-6

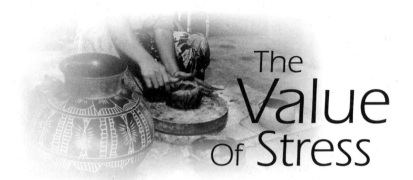

The Value of Stress

Our two boys love history. But they hate tours. In fact, they have managed to make the word *tour* into two very long syllables. "Daddy," they moan pitifully, "are we going on a tooooooo-ur?" When I assured them one summer morning we were going to see a working early-American town, not just costumed ladies telling about old buildings, they consented. Cautiously.

The craftsmen made the place come alive. The blacksmith worked his magic with fire and iron. The miller showed us how a waterwheel and some wheat equals flour. And the potter made us forget any leftover impressions of a "tooooooo-ur." His skill was almost hypnotic. He sat at his wheel, rhythmically turning the shaft with his feet. In a nearby corner were shapeless, seemingly worthless gray blobs of clay. One of those former blobs was now the focus of all his attention. With practiced fingers the potter was working that clay upward into a smooth and shapely vase.

The potter's shack was cramped, too small for all the people crowded in to watch on that hot day. Eventually, the crowd left. But our kids wanted to stay. They had noticed two shelves of finished vases, one on either side of the potter. With childlike innocence one of my young sons reached out to touch.

"Careful!" the craftsman exclaimed. "Please don't touch the pottery on that shelf. You'll ruin it." Then he surprised us when he said, "Why don't you touch the ones on the other shelf?" Needless to say, we were curious why some vases could be touched and not others.

Glancing at the "do-not-touch" shelf, he explained, "These haven't been fired yet." The potter told us then that there was more to making masterpieces than just making blobs into beautiful shapes. If he stopped at that point, they would quickly be marred and misshapen. Without the fire, the potter's work is still beautiful, but too fragile.

Without the fire, the potter's work is still beautiful, but too fragile.

The other vases could be touched because they had twice been baked in his kiln at temperatures of more than 2,000 degrees. "The fire makes the clay firm and strong," our host concluded. "Fire makes the beauty last." That was the trigger. My thoughts raced to Peter's words in 1 Peter 1:6-7:

> *All kinds of trials . . . have come so that your faith—of greater worth than gold, which perishes even though refined by fire—may be proved genuine.*

Both Peter and the potter were talking to me about a fire that increases the value of something precious. Having spent most of my adult years in an oven—a pressure cooker, to be exact—I knew about fire. Much of it could be traced to my overheated schedule and overcommitted lifestyle. That heat was my own fault.

But there is another fire that comes not from me but from the Master Potter. There is, to be sure, a heat that burns, and another heat that beautifies.

God- Produced Stress

From the first day that I discovered the verse "Seek peace and pursue it" (Ps. 34:14), I hoped that my life would slow down. It hasn't, but I have. By removing some roots of my restlessness, I have performed surgery on the stress that comes from me. By attacking stress-centers in my life, I am managing the stress that's coming at me . . . and there is still plenty left! That's because there is supposed to be. What keeps pushing on me is the heavenly stress that is for me—the heat that time proves, strengthens, and beautifies.

Personal peace is not the elimination of stress. If we live without pressure, we are as fragile as that potter's unfired vase. God has been skillfully reshaping me on His wheel, making a "blob" into something far more valuable. But that workmanship needs fire to make it firm and strong.

In pursuing peace, I am trying to eliminate the stress that I cause and to control that which others cause. What's left is the stress that God Himself either causes or allows. Peace-living resists self-induced stress but grows from God-produced stress.

If the pressure is taken off a piece of coal, there will be no diamond. Removing that irritating grain of sand from an oyster's tummy means having no pearl. Protecting an apple tree from the pain of the pruning knife results in little fruit. Pressure, irritation, and pain can be tools to develop people too.

It's the wrong kind of pressure that can crush or weaken or kill. That is where my "gerbil-wheel" life had created an overload. Even with much of that unloaded now, my days still get crunched with plenty of demands, changes, and frustrations. While the weight is as much as ever, it just doesn't seem as heavy. God may send a load. But He will never send an overload.

As my stress-weary heart has followed the word *peace* through the Bible, I uncovered this perspective on my pressures:

> *Endure hardship as discipline; God is treating you as sons. . . . No discipline seems pleasant at the time, but painful. Later on, however, it produces a harvest of righteousness and peace for those who have been trained by it (Heb. 12:7,11).*

There it is! Stress that contributes to our peace! Hardship here is defined as training. But if we are not looking for the trainer's lesson in the problem, we get only the pain and miss the peace. When a peace-pursuer understands he is in training rather than in trouble, he can relax even under fire. Knowing that peace will come from this pain doesn't make the pain any more enjoyable, but you can handle it calmly.

God may send a load, but He will never send an overload.

Frankly, I almost lost my personal peace before it was even a month old. My "showdown with stress" had come at the end of the summer. I came away from my turning point with a fresh sense of hope, sensing I had finally regained control. I had made specific commitments to my Lord, my wife, my children, and my work—commitments based on the biblical description of a peaceful life. That's when everything started to unravel.

I expected fall to be a circus as usual, getting three children acclimated in three different schools, managing the high-energy startup of another school year in youth ministry, a heavy schedule of speaking and meetings.

I entered the fall fray joyful, expectant, and confident. I had learned to practice peace. I did not expect the avalanche on top of the circus. It started late in September at a local high school football game. I was grabbed by a friend who blurted out, "I think your son has a broken arm." It took only a look at Doug to confirm the bad news.

I will never forget the scene that followed in the emergency room. Because both bones were broken and twisted, the doctor had to probe and push and pull for a long time. Doug was brave, but his pain was almost unbearable. Strangely, in a way only a parent could understand, so was mine. When we finally got home, Karen and I agreed that we felt totally depleted—as if we each had broken an arm.

The emotional struggle lasted a lot longer than the physical pain. A broken arm may not rate very high on a chart of human suffering, but it is a heavy burden for an athletic 12-year-old boy. All of his fall sports dreams were shattered by his broken arm. His natural self-consciousness about beginning junior high was complicated by 4 months in a cast. Doug's favorite seasons—Halloween through Thanksgiving, Christmas, and New Year's—evaporated as his friends ran hard and he laid low. When the doctor later announced that the bones were healing crooked, we realized this battle could actually last for years, not months. There were tremors in my new peace.

> **When the doctor later announced that the bones were healing crooked,**
> **. . . there were tremors in my new peace.**

That broken arm turned out to be only the opening shot in a barrage of new tensions. The night Karen and I returned from Haiti, she was seized with a severe gastrointestinal attack. Unable to move, Karen had to be rushed to the hospital by ambulance before our bags were even unpacked. Her pain was so severe that our family doctor stayed most of the night with us. It was the second time in 2 weeks that I had stood in this same emergency room, watching someone I love suffer.

This was to be followed by Karen's dangerous attack of phlebitis, forcing her to bed when we were running full speed together to finish a major project. By the time the hepatitis put her in bed for 6 months, we either had to laugh or cry. We did some of each. Just for good measure, we threw in a week in the hospital for our daughter too. The tremors were beginning to register higher on the Richter scale.

With things at home up for grabs, it would have helped if things at work were stable. They weren't. It was at this same time that we faced a severe cash crisis. It threatened to paralyze us. Our people were not complaining, but they were not being paid on time. Simultaneously, some unresolved personnel conflicts surfaced, threatening to pull us apart. The long meetings that ensued led to new stresses of some major reorganization. The frosting came with our landlord's notice—he had sold our office building and we would have to move!

God allowed me to be caught in an avalanche of friendly stress.

By now, I had a major "peacequake" reeling inside me. Just when I was trying to simplify my life, it got more complicated. I found myself on my knees asking, "God, if You want me to pursue personal peace, why is all this happening? You aren't even giving me a chance!"

Actually, a chance for peace is exactly what God was giving me. These upheavals were forcing me to rearrange misplaced priorities, some I would never have seen any other way. Unhealthy dependencies were being broken, as "asking Ron" was becoming more difficult. I was unintentionally less available because of the fires I was fighting. And I was driven closer to my Lord than ever before. Since He is the ultimate source of peace, I began to taste that "peace of God, which transcends all understanding" (Phil. 4:7).

God allowed me to be caught in an avalanche of friendly stress. He was helping me, driving me, to reorganize my life around saner expectations. And the tests had not taken my peace—they had confirmed it. God was speaking through this whirlwind to say, "This peace of Mine is stronger than you thought!"

STUDY NO. 2

Under-standing Stress
(Part 1)

Psalm 34:14—"Depart
from evil and do good;
seek peace and pursue it."

Objective:
**To see how God
can use stress to
build our lives.**

Bible Memorization:
Psalm 34:14

Read:
**"The Value Of
Stress" & "God-
Produced Stress"
pp.12-17**

Warming Up
It is often hard to see stress as a positive or valuable
thing. What kinds of stress are positive, and what kinds
seem more like a burden?

Thinking Through
The illustration of the potter and his oven is an
interesting way to view stress (see pp.12-13). How did
the heat affect the vases? How does the "heat" of stress
affect you?

"God may send a load, but He will never send an
overload" (p.15). What does this mean? How is this an
encouragement to you?

How can God often be the source of both stress and
peace? (see pp.16-17).

Digging In
Key Text: Hebrews 12:7-11
Why is chastening often characteristic of God's dealings
with His true children? In what ways does this parallel
the dealings of a parent with a child?

According to v.10, what is God's ultimate goal in chastening His child? Why is that goal so important for our Christian experience?

In what ways (v.11) does the present experience of chastening differ from its intended result?

Going Further
Refer
This lesson's memory verse, Psalm 34:14, calls us to the pursuit of peace. How can we seek and pursue peace? How does that parallel the pursuit of "good" instead of evil?

Reflect
List and identify the stresses in your life under the three categories—self-induced stress, stress caused by others, and God-produced stress. To what extent can you eliminate the self-induced stress and stress caused by others?

As you close this lesson, spend some time in prayer asking for God's protection from your own self-induced stress and seeking His loving hand of correction where it is needed in your life. When finished, record what you prayed for.

"⁷If you endure chastening, God deals with you as with sons; for what son is there whom a father does not chasten? ⁸But if you are without chastening, of which all have become partakers, then you are illegitimate and not sons. ⁹Furthermore, we have had human fathers who corrected us, and we paid them respect. Shall we not much more readily be in subjection to the Father of spirits and live? ¹⁰For they indeed for a few days chastened us as seemed best to them, but He for our profit, that we may be partakers of His holiness. ¹¹Now no chastening seems to be joyful for the present, but painful; nevertheless, afterward it yields the peaceable fruit of righteousness to those who have been trained by it."
Hebrews 12:7-11

Father- Filtered Stress

There's another stress that God doesn't send but allows. Job is a dramatic example of this. The Bible says that all his losses and suffering were Satan's idea, calculated to disillusion his faith in God. Yet even the devil cannot bring pressure and pain without God's permission!

A unique behind-the-scenes look at spiritual warfare emerges from Job's predicament. Satan could not touch Job until God okayed it. Satan approached God, asking to go beyond the "hedge around him and his household" (Job 1:10). The Lord gave a conditional yes when He answered, "Very well, then, everything he has is in your hands, but on the man himself do not lay a finger" (v.12).

Job's glue through his personal holocaust was a faith that declared, "Shall we accept good from God, and not trouble? . . . The Lord gave and the Lord has taken away; may the name of the Lord be praised" (2:10; 1:21). His analysis was, at best, only partially right. Actually, the devil had "taken away" and sent the "trouble." But Job trusted in a Father who knows what is best for His children, and that He had to okay these trials somewhere along the way.

Job's troubles make ours look like pinpricks. Still, I have found myself asking during our recent avalanches, "Is God trying to build us, or is Satan trying to bury us?" Since that's virtually unanswerable, I have decided to ask a better question, "How can God use this?" If this pressure could not train me, the Coach would not allow it. Our problems look much less terrifying when we realize they are Father-filtered. That filtering is guaranteed in promises such as "God is faithful; He will not let you be tempted beyond what you can bear" (1 Cor. 10:13).

In other words, nothing can enter the life of God's child without His signature. His approval is based on what we can bear. He will allow us to be pushed to the building point, but not the breaking point. It's a little like weightlifting. Too much weight will crush us, but greater weight than we have lifted before is needed to make us stronger. Only the Lord knows the difference, and He filters every additional load.

Everywhere the apostle Paul traveled, he was relentlessly tormented by his unnamed thorn in the flesh (2 Cor. 12:7). He identified its source as "a messenger of Satan." In spite of the devilish origin of his trouble, he looked for the lesson— a reason his Father would allow it. Paul concluded that his thorn was sent "to keep me from becoming conceited . . . that Christ's power may rest on me" (2 Cor. 12:7,9).

God will allow us to be pushed to the building point, but not to the breaking point.

That same pressured preacher also looked for the Lord in his trouble and sensed His comfort and assurance when He said, "My grace is sufficient for you, for My power is made perfect in weakness" (v.9).

⚙️

Understanding Stress
(Part 2)

2 Cor.12:9—"And He said to me, 'My grace is sufficient for you, for My strength is made perfect in weakness.' Therefore most gladly I will rather boast in my infirmities, that the power of Christ may rest upon me."

Objective:
To understand God's protection in times of stress.

Bible Memorization:
2 Corinthians 12:9

Read:
**"Father-Filtered Stress"
pp.20-21**

Warming Up
In your own household, what kinds of things get "filtered"? In what ways is this helpful? How are those filtered things improved by that process?

Thinking Through
What is the difference between what God "sends" and what God "allows"? (see p.20). In the example of Job, how did God limit what Satan was allowed to do?

On page 21, we read that "nothing can enter the life of God's child without His signature." According to the lesson, on what does God base His approval? How can knowing this give us comfort in difficult times?

On page 21, we are offered the confidence that "God will allow us to be pushed to the building point, but not to the breaking point." What are these two points? What is the basis for this confidence?

Digging In
Key Text: 2 Corinthians 12:7-10
What do you think was Paul's "thorn in the flesh"? (v.7). Why was it given? How can Paul say that this thorn was both a gift from God and a "messenger of Satan"? (v.7). Why is this not contradictory?

Why do we need to be brought to a point of weakness to experience God's strength? (v.9). What was Paul's response to this weakness? Why did he respond that way?

What caused Paul to "take pleasure"? (v.10). Why? Does that response seem reasonable or unreasonable to you? Why?

Going Further
Refer
From this lesson's reading, how would you see Paul's and Job's experiences as similar? How are they different?

Reflect
When have you felt overwhelmed by the challenges in your life? How did you respond to those burdens? How do you think God used those burdens to help you grow?

What are some challenges you are currently facing? How might God be filtering them for your good? How can you submit them to Him more completely?

"7And lest I should be exalted above measure by the abundance of the revelations, a thorn in the flesh was given to me, a messenger of Satan to buffet me, lest I be exalted above measure. 8Concerning this thing I pleaded with the Lord three times that it might depart from me. 9And He said to me, 'My grace is sufficient for you, for My strength is made perfect in weakness.' Therefore most gladly I will rather boast in my infirmities, that the power of Christ may rest upon me. 10Therefore I take pleasure in infirmities, in reproaches, in needs, in persecutions, in distresses, for Christ's sake. For when I am weak, then I am strong."

2 Corinthians 12:7-10

Surviving
The Storms
of Stress

Amid all the hoopla of the 1984 Summer Olympics in Los Angeles, one tragic casualty was generally overlooked. Boomer didn't make it. In the extravagant opening ceremonies, a bald eagle named Boomer was scheduled to soar into the Coliseum to the strains of "America The Beautiful." Unfortunately, Boomer was unable to show up for his performance. Three days before the Olympics opened, Boomer died—of stress, they said. I guess even an eagle can tell when things are out of hand. People-pressure was just too much for the old bird. He knew how to survive the dangers of the wilderness but not the stresses of civilization.

We can sympathize with poor Boomer. We all have those crushing moments when we feel as if we're dying of stress. Recent medical research tells us that many people are literally killed by stress. For the rest of us who feel the punishment of emotional dying, survival skills become crucial.

Establishing quiet centers and peaceful habits give us precious resources for inner peace. When we attack the roots of stress in us and the chronic stress centers around us, we make room for the friendly stress that will always be there. But even with that plan for peace in place, there is one important item of unfinished business. How do we handle the rest of the mess—the circumstances beyond our control?

There are important answers in the account of the most violent storm experienced in the New Testament. Acts 27 describes the savage nor'easter that threatened the ship transporting Paul to trial in Rome. They lost all control of their circumstances—yet they survived. And locked inside this storm-tossed story are the four skills we need to survive the unavoidable storms of stress.

Get Rid
Of The
Cargo
You Don't Need

Luke, the author of Acts, explains the first survival skill in this way:

We took such a violent battering from the storm that the next day they began to throw the cargo overboard. . . . with their own hands (Acts 27:18-19).

If someone had suggested to the captain of the ship upon departure that the cargo, the ship's tackle, and maybe even his favorite chair were going overboard, he probably would have burned their ears with his reply. Yet when the storm hit, they decided they could do without some items they once were sure they needed.

It takes a storm to make us consider even letting go.

If we are going to handle our own personal nor'easters, we will have to get rid of the cargo we do not need. Of course, it sometimes takes a storm to make us even consider letting go.

Some of our "extra cargo" may be bad things we have accumulated like barnacles: a compromising relationship, deepening debt, a growing obsession with money, an entangling sinful habit, a critical attitude—things we hang on to until a storm exposes how they are sinking us.

There is good cargo too that may have to be jettisoned. We tend to

25

accumulate involvements that, taken separately, are each neutral—even helpful. But taken together, they are just too much.

A storm is our chance to change. When the rough weather subsides, we can return to the same overloaded or wrongly loaded lifestyle. That in turn could set the stage for an even bigger storm. If you want to survive your personal "hurricane," evaluate extra cargo and get rid of it before it sinks you—one way or another.

Get Busy
With The
Things
That Really Matter

Luke tells us that "Hurricane Paul" lasted 2 weeks! Then an angel appeared to Paul in the middle of the night. Paul's visitor introduced a second survival skill for a storm. The apostle announced this message to the crew:

> Not one of you will be lost; only the ship will be destroyed. Last night an angel of the God whose I am and whom I serve stood beside me and said, . . . "God has graciously given you the lives of all who sail with you" (Acts 27:22-24).

In essence, the angel had simply reminded Paul, "The ship doesn't matter. Only the people do." To survive a storm you get busy with the things that really matter—and those "things" are usually people! With all the pressures to achieve and accomplish, the people we love can slowly get pushed to the corners of our lives.

Neglect is not intentional—weeds grow in our garden, not because we plant them but because we forget them. Many a man leaves a wife or a child in his dust as he speeds toward his career goals. Many a woman slowly vanishes from the most important moments of her loved ones as she loses herself in a job, a social circle, a religious responsibility. Co-workers or employees can become functions instead of people with needs.

It usually takes a storm to restore our values.

Without realizing it, we let those close to us become simply dispensers of information, transportation, hugs, money, or services. It usually takes a storm to restore our values.

In the pursuit of peace, the "ship"—the project, the schedule, the deadline, the organization, the budget—may be lost on the rocks. That is costly, but it's okay. It is our people we cannot afford to lose. If the storm blows you back to them, you have all you really need. You can always find another ship.

STUDY
NO.

4

Surviving
The Storms Of
Stress
(Part 1)

1 Corinthians 10:13—"No temptation has overtaken you except such as is common to man; but God is faithful, who will not allow you to be tempted beyond what you are able, but with the temptation will also make the way of escape, that you may be able to bear it."

Objective:
To begin to practice wise responses to stress.

Bible Memorization:
1 Corinthians 10:13

Read:
"Surviving Storms," "Get Rid Of Cargo," & "Get Busy With Things That Matter"
pp.24-27

Warming Up
Have you ever been in a ship during a storm? If not, what kind of experience could you relate to that would produce a similar sense of insecurity and fear?

Thinking Through
On page 25, we read about the need to "get rid of the cargo" to save the ship. What examples of "cargo" in our lives does the lesson offer? Which do you relate to the most? Why?

How can unintentional neglect (see p.27) creep into our lives and impact our relationship with God? Our relationships with others?

Would you agree or disagree that what really matters in life are people? (p.27). Why? Who matters to you? Why is each significant to you?

Digging In
Key Text: Acts 27:20-25
How does v.20 describe the severity of the storm Paul and his shipmates faced? How did it impact them? Why?

Twice in the key text Paul encourages the sailors to "take heart." Why would it be difficult to "take heart" when faced with the danger they were in?

How do you think the sailors reacted to Paul's two calls "to take heart"? (vv.22,25). What is the basis of his confidence? How do you take heart in the midst of a helpless situation?

Going Further
Refer
In this lesson's memory verse (1 Corinthians 10:13), we read about God's care for His child during stressful times. What are the elements of that care, and why are they rooted in the character of God Himself?

Reflect
What types of "cargo" are you hanging on to that may be bringing unnecessary pressure on your life and/or relationships? In what ways can you respond to "right the ship" of your personal priorities?

Are there people in your life you have neglected by shifting your priorities to the "cargo"? Is God one of those persons? How can you begin today to seek forgiveness and restore those relationships?

"[20]Now when neither sun nor stars appeared for many days, and no small tempest beat on us, all hope that we would be saved was finally given up. [21]But after long abstinence from food, then Paul stood in the midst of them and said, "Men, you should have listened to me, and not have sailed from Crete and incurred this disaster and loss. [22]And now I urge you to take heart, for there will be no loss of life among you, but only of the ship. [23]For there stood by me this night an angel of the God to whom I belong and whom I serve, [24]saying, 'Do not be afraid, Paul; you must be brought before Caesar; and indeed God has granted you all those who sail with you.' [25]Therefore take heart, men, for I believe God that it will be just as it was told me."

Acts 27:20-25

Get Desperate With God

Our faith tends to be cool, calm, and collected—until a crisis clobbers us. Then we go from our feet to our knees, and God becomes more than someone who "helps" us: He is our only hope.

Luke apparently spoke for himself, and Paul too, when he said, "We finally gave up all hope of being saved" (Acts 27:20). That is probably why the visiting angel greeted Paul by announcing, "Do not be afraid, Paul" (v.24).

I'm glad for that glimpse of the apostle's humanity. He is on such a pedestal in my mind that I would expect to find him standing bravely in the bow of the boat, like George Washington crossing the Delaware. Instead, Paul seems to be as terrified as everyone else—and as desperate. In his desperation he was met by "the God whose I am and whom I serve" (v.23).

Paul models for us a third survival skill in a storm—getting desperate with God. When the bottom drops out, it is easy to get desperate. The sailors on Paul's ship sensed that they were headed for the rocks. So . . .

> In an attempt to escape from the ship, the sailors let the lifeboat down into the sea . . . . Then Paul said, . . . "Unless these men stay with the ship, you cannot be saved." So the soldiers cut the ropes that held the lifeboat and let it fall away (vv.30-32).

Often our panic makes us reach for a lifeboat instead of the Lord. My lifeboats have usually just made bigger messes. I have hired the wrong people, spent unwisely, cut programs too soon, pushed people I love too hard. A storm can make us panic or make us pray.

It is when our points of reference disappear like the sailors' stars that we learn what prayer really means. Stripped of any possibility of self-rescue, we throw ourselves on the Lord. Our praying is not controlled, predictable, third person; we finally open our religious hand and let God fill it with something supernatural.

At certain points in your life with Him, God will strip you of all other resources, leaving you only Himself. Then you will discover, in the words of a wise old saint, "You never know Jesus is all you need until Jesus is all you've got."

Often our panic makes us reach for a lifeboat instead of the Lord. . . .
A storm can make us panic or make us pray.

And then there is peace, no matter how long the storm lasts. In the words of King David, you can proclaim:

When anxiety was great within me, Your consolation brought joy to my soul (Ps. 94:19).

Get Back To
^AHealthy
Routine

When the boat is headed for the rocks, lunch can wait. Yet as Paul's ship was about to go aground, he urged the crew to eat. "For the last fourteen days," he said, "you have been in constant suspense and have gone without food . . . . Now I urge you to take some food. You need it to survive" (Acts 27:33-34).

Paul advocated here a fourth survival skill in a storm—getting back to a healthy routine. When a strong disturbance batters our ship, our daily routines are usually the first things thrown overboard. In reality, the heavier the pressure, the more important it is to guard our sources of strength.

When we start to miss sleep, meals, and breaks, we start sinking. Quiet centers tend to be neglected when we start cutting corners. More than ever, we have to fight for that quality time with our Lord, our lovers, and little ones. Those healthy routines are what keep us strong on both sunny and stormy days.

Blown Where You Belong

There's a line from an old hymn that beautifully interprets the storms we face:

> Clouds arise and tempests blow
> By order from Thy throne.

When God orders up a tempest in my life, it is because a change is needed. Usually, the storm is not the real issue—not from God's viewpoint. It is an imbalance that has developed in my priorities, a dislocation so subtle that I can't even see it until turbulence gets my attention.

It is in storms that I literally get blown back in balance. I am learning not to throw that wonderful new peace overboard when my ship spins out of control. It is, instead, time to get rid of the cargo I do not need, get busy with the things that really matter, get desperate with God, and get back to a healthy routine. God has provided that positive strategy for weathering the storms of friendly stress.

The account of Hurricane Paul ends with a thrilling postscript. Luke records that the tempest finally blew them aground on the island of Malta. One look at a map reveals what was really happening in the midst of that raging crisis at sea. Malta sits right off the southern coast of Italy, the ship's original destination! The whole time they thought they were out of control, they were right on course!

Our plans may be interrupted by storms, but God's plans never are. In fact, the storm is part of His plan.

Centuries before, the ancient Jewish prophet Nahum said it all in a simple sentence: "His way is in the whirlwind and the storm" (Nah. 1:3).

Our plans may be interrupted by storms, but God's plans never are. In fact, the storm is part of His plan. If we don't abandon ship, the winds of God will blow us right where we belong—no matter how off course we feel.

STUDY NO. 5

Surviving
The Storms of
Stress
(Part 2)

Psalm 94:19—"In the multitude of my anxieties within me, Your comforts delight my soul."

Objective:
To begin to practice wise responses to stress.

Bible Memorization:
Psalm 94:19

Read:
"Get Desperate With God" & "Get Back To A Healthy Routine" pp.30-33

Warming Up
"Desperate times call for desperate measures." What are some choices you have made in past crises that would qualify as "desperate measures"?

Thinking Through
We are reminded (p.31) that often "our panic makes us reach for a lifeboat instead of the Lord." What "lifeboats" might get in the way of your trusting the Lord in a time of crisis?

How is getting back to a healthy routine (pp.32-33) a survival skill? What would constitute "a healthy routine" for you?

The author speaks of "quiet centers" that have been neglected (p.32). What does he mean by "quiet centers"? Why would getting back to these centers help us survive in a storm?

Digging In
Key Text: Acts 27:30-36
How did the soldiers respond to Paul's warning in v.31? Why do you think they believed his words? Would you have believed him?

Was it sensible for Paul to tell the sailors not to take the lifeboats when the ship seemed to be sinking? (v.31). What gave Paul the confidence to say that?

Notice Paul's bold yet subtle witness to these sailors and soldiers (v.35). What did he do, and what was the impact of his actions?

Going Further
Refer
Compare the psalmist's feelings in the first part of Psalm 94:19 ("multitude of anxieties") with his response in the second part ("delight my soul"). What made the difference? How does that compare to the events in Acts 27:30-36?

Reflect
"You never know Jesus is all you need until Jesus is all you've got" (p.31). What does this mean? In what ways have you been brought to such a point?

List some "quiet centers" you need to get back into at this time. What must you do to reclaim these quiet centers for yourself?

"³⁰And as the sailors were seeking to escape from the ship, when they had let down the skiff into the sea, under pretense of putting out anchors from the prow, ³¹Paul said to the centurion and the soldiers, 'Unless these men stay in the ship, you cannot be saved.' ³²Then the soldiers cut away the ropes of the skiff and let it fall off. ³³And as day was about to dawn, Paul implored them all to take food, saying, 'Today is the fourteenth day you have waited and continued without food, and eaten nothing. ³⁴Therefore I urge you to take nourishment, for this is for your survival, since not a hair will fall from the head of any of you.' ³⁵And when he had said these things, he took bread and gave thanks to God in the presence of them all; and when he had broken it he began to eat. ³⁶Then they were all encouraged, and also took food themselves."
Acts 27:30-36

Coping
Isn't
Enough

Nancy's "glass of stress" is full and overflowing. Wedged between the demands of single-parenting, a rebellious son, and managing an office, she has just about had it. When she heard that I was writing about peace and stress, she said, "Oh, I'm reading something right now about how to cope with stress. I hope I find out in time!"

Most of us pressure-cooker people would, like Nancy, consider it success just to cope with our stress. But after years of coping, I have decided that coping is not enough.

According to the dictionary, to cope is "to struggle or contend on fairly even terms." That sounds like treading water but never getting to shore! Since my stress-saturated life did not drown me, I guess I was coping. But just keeping our heads above water leaves us vulnerable to any big wave that comes along.

When I made a commitment to go after peace, I wanted to learn to conquer stress, not just cope with it. Stress was too often dredging up my dark side, subverting our family life, shuffling sane priorities. I hungered for a peace that would break its grip.

I found it in a promise in the Bible that has been tested by two millennia of believers. The apostle Paul had the credentials to pen the words; turbulence and upheaval had been a way of life for him. Just before the promise, he listed every major disturbance in the human experience: trouble, hardship, persecution, famine, nakedness, danger, sword, death (Rom. 8:35-36).

Then, with this catalog of life's storms in mind he proclaimed:

In all these things we are more than conquerors through Him who loved us (Rom. 8:37).

If we can be "more than conquerors" in the stresses of life, why should we settle for coping?

The difference between coping and conquering seems to be those two little words—"through Him." Without them, this is just another inspiring way to say, "Think positively." Real personal peace is not the result of positive thinking.

Peace
Is Ultimately
A Person

The ancient Jewish prophets called Him "the Prince of Peace." When Jesus came, the Christmas angels promised He would be a Savior whose saving would bring peace. When He left, He promised:

Peace I leave with you; My peace I give you (Jn. 14:27).

His servant Paul summed it up when he reminded us:

He came and preached peace to you who were far away and peace to those who were near (Eph. 2:17).

Then, in six simple words, he spoke the prescription for peace:

For He Himself is our peace (Eph. 2:14).

I was one of those Paul described as "those who were near." Years ago, I had recognized that the war in my heart was really a battle with God. I realized that I could not have Christ's peace until He was my Prince. Opening the hands that had so tightly gripped the steering wheel of my life, I let Jesus drive.

Since we were made to live for the God who made us, everything else is out of place until we find Him. And He can only be found at the cross, where His Son paid the bill for our war against God. Whether we have rejected God, or simply neglected Him, the result is the same—a life He made and paid for, lived without Him. Upon our invitation, He enters our lives—bringing His peace.

Since my personal visit to Jesus' cross, I have known the Person who is peace. Through the most turbulent stress seasons, I have been unsinkable, as Paul said, "through Him who loved us" (Rom. 8:37). His pressure on the inside has always been greater than the pressure on the outside.

I was like a man with an inexhaustible bank account who wasn't writing many checks on it.

But for so long, I have been something much less than "more than a conqueror." My complicated lifestyle had allowed too many other hands on that steering wheel. I wasn't crashing, but I was swerving. Then the prison cell door swung open, and my Rescuer said, "Seek peace and pursue it."

I have been pursuing it ever since. The peace I hungered for has been there since Christ came in. But I was like a man with an inexhaustible bank account who wasn't writing many checks on it. The poverty, the pressure of my life, was waiting for peace to come instead of going after it.

Inner peace is the natural condition of the heart in which Christ lives. I just need to quit blocking and sabotaging the supply lines.

In a sense, my search for peace ends where it began. Years ago I came to Christ for peace. Years later, I am learning to enjoy it by discovering Him more deeply than ever before. The pursuit of peace is ultimately the pursuit of a Person.

The gales of stress have blown me to the Prince of Peace. And just as Paul was carried to God's destination by that nor'easter, He may be using the storms of your life to drive you to Him.

Inner peace is the natural quality of the heart in which Christ lives.

If the load you are carrying seems too heavy for you, it is because you were never meant to carry it alone. Coping may well be a touch-and-go struggle, but conquering is totally out of your reach. Stress is eroding even your ability to cope.

That moment of extremity is His opportunity. Strangely enough, you may be closer to peace than you have ever been, and the stress of your life has carried you there. We stand tired of fighting—and Jesus quietly whispers, "Come to Me, all you who are weary and burdened, and I will give you rest" (Mt. 11:28).

Strong and proud, we don't feel the need, even though it is just as urgent then. But battered and wounded by years of battle, we know we need help—the rest. That's when our hand reaches for His. Peace is a Person—and peace rooted in Him can triumphantly stand any test.

STUDY
NO. 6

Surviving
The Storms Of
Stress
(Part 3)

John 14:27—"Peace I leave with you, My peace I give to you; not as the world gives do I give to you. Let not your heart be troubled, neither let it be afraid."

Objective:
To begin to practice wise responses to stress.

Bible Memorization:
John 14:27

Read:
**"Coping Isn't Enough" & "Peace Is Ultimately A Person"
pp.36-39**

Warming Up
Sometimes when troubles come, we try to "cope," that is, to survive. What are some coping mechanisms people might use in a time of serious trials?

Thinking Through
On page 36 we read, "After years of coping, I have decided that coping is not enough." Why is coping not an appropriate solution to tough times? What impact might "coping" have on your stress levels?

"Real personal peace is not the result of positive thinking" (p.37). Do you agree or disagree with this statement? Why?

On page 38 we see the bold statement, "Inner peace is the natural condition of the heart in which Christ lives." Why is the presence of Christ so critical to experiencing peace of mind?

Digging In
Key Text: Romans 8:35-39
In v.35, what does Paul say is unable to separate us from God's love? How do these issues relate to life in the 21st century?

What does Paul say can make sheep headed for slaughter into victorious conquerors? (vv.36-37). How can that assurance of victory bring comfort to our hearts?

In vv.38-39, Paul gives a more comprehensive list of all that cannot separate us from God's love. What are they and, taken together, what do they represent?

Going Further
Refer
Compare the trials in Romans 8:35-39 to Christ's words in John 14:27 (this lesson's memory verse). How do the two texts combine to offer hope during stressful situations?

Reflect
What have you learned in this study that will help you as you face storms of stress?

How has this study helped you to trust God and to protect relationships when stress strikes? Commit in prayer that you will move beyond coping into a trusting relationship with God—even to the point of trusting Him with your points of stress.

"[35]Who shall separate us from the love of Christ? Shall tribulation, or distress, or persecution, or famine, or nakedness, or peril, or sword? [36]As it is written: 'For Your sake we are killed all day long; we are accounted as sheep for the slaughter.' [37]Yet in all these things we are more than conquerors through Him who loved us. [38]For I am persuaded that neither death nor life, nor angels nor principalities nor powers, nor things present nor things to come, [39]nor height nor depth, nor any other created thing, shall be able to separate us from the love of God which is in Christ Jesus our Lord."
Romans 8:35-39

Peace
In The
Storms

Corrie ten Boom testified to God's peace from the greatest hell that man could create—the Nazi concentration camps of World War II. She and her dear sister Betsie paid the price for hiding Jews in the attic of their home in Holland. Through torture, humiliation, and pain, they turned to the Christ who lived in them—and tested His peace. Their witness was backed by the credentials of a suffering that few of us have ever known.

Betsie died in that concentration camp; Corrie was released as a result of a clerical error. In Betsie's dying hours, she spoke a message that Corrie would carry around the world for nearly 40 years. Betsie said, "Tell them that there is no pit so deep but that God's love is deeper still."

Corrie and her sister had tasted what it means to be "more than conquerors through Him who loved us." The peace that Christ brings is that strong.

If our stress makes us hungry for His peace, then it has driven us home. The storm has blown us into the Harbor that we have looked for all our lives.

Discovery Series Bible Study
Leader's And User's Guide

Statement Of Purpose

The *Discovery Series Bible Study* (DSBS) series provides assistance to pastors and leaders in discipling and teaching Christians through the use of RBC Ministries *Discovery Series* booklets. The DSBS series uses the inductive Bible-study method to help Christians understand the Bible more clearly.

Study Helps

Listed at the beginning of each study are the key verse, objective, and memorization verses. These will act as the compass and map for each study.

Some key Bible passages are printed out fully. This will help the students to focus on these passages and to examine and compare the Bible texts more easily— leading to a better understanding of their meanings. Serious students are encouraged to open their own Bible to examine the other Scriptures as well.

How To Use DSBS (for individuals and small groups)

Individuals—Personal Study

- Read the designated pages of the book.
- Carefully consider and answer all the questions.

Small Groups—Bible-Study Discussion

- To maximize the value of the time spent together, each member should do the lesson work prior to the group meeting.
- Recommended discussion time: 45–55 minutes.
- Engage the group in a discussion of the questions, seeking full participation from each of the members.

Overview Of Lessons

Study	Topic	Bible Text	Reading	Questions
1	Creating Stress	1 Tim. 6:6-10	pp.5-9	pp.10-11
2	Understanding Stress (pt.1)	Heb. 12:7-11	pp.12-17	pp.18-19
3	Understanding Stress (pt.2)	2 Cor. 12:7-10	pp.20-21	pp.22-23
4	Surviving The Storms Of Stress (pt.1)	Acts 27:20-25	pp.24-27	pp.28-29
5	Surviving The Storms Of Stress (pt.2)	Acts 27:30-36	pp.30-33	pp.34-35
6	Surviving The Storms Of Stress (pt.3)	Rom. 8:35-39	pp.36-39	pp.40-41

The DSBS format incorporates a "layered" approach to Bible study that includes four segments. These segments form a series of perspectives that become increasingly more personalized and focused. These segments are:

Warming Up. In this section, a general interest question is used to begin the discussion (in small groups) or "to get the juices flowing" (in personal study). It is intended to begin the process of interaction at the broadest, most general level.

Thinking Through. Here, the student or group is invited to interact with the *Discovery Series* material that has been read. In considering the information and implications of the booklet, these questions help to drive home the critical concepts of that portion of the booklet.

Digging In. Moving away from the *Discovery Series* material, this section isolates a key biblical text from the manuscript and engages the student or group in a brief inductive study of that passage of Scripture. This brings the authority of the Bible into the forefront of the study as we consider its message to our hearts and lives.

Going Further. This final segment contains two parts. In *Refer*, the student or group has the opportunity to test the ideas of the lesson against the rest of the Bible by cross-referencing the text with other verses. In *Reflect*, the student or group is challenged to personally apply the lesson by making a practical response to what has been learned.

Pulpit Sermon Series (for pastors and church leaders)

Although the *Discovery Series Bible Study* is primarily for personal and group study, pastors may want to use this material as the foundation for a series of messages on this important issue. The suggested topics and their corresponding texts are as follows:

Sermon No.	Topic	Text
1	Creating Stress	1 Tim. 6:6-10
2	Understanding Stress (Part 1)	Heb. 12:7-11
3	Understanding Stress (Part 2)	2 Cor. 12:7-10
4	Surviving The Storms Of Stress (Part 1)	Acts 27:20-25
5	Surviving The Storms Of Stress (Part 2)	Acts 27:30-36
6	Surviving The Storms Of Stress (Part 3)	Rom. 8:35-39

Final Thoughts

The DSBS will provide an opportunity for growth and ministry. To internalize the spiritual truths of each study in a variety of environments, the material is arranged to allow for flexibility in the application of the truths discussed.

Whether DSBS is used in small-group Bible studies, adult Sunday school classes, adult Bible fellowships, men's and women's study groups, or church-wide applications, the key to the strength of the discussion will be found in the preparation of each participant. Likewise, the effectiveness of personal and pastoral use of this material will be directly related to the time committed to using this resource.

As you use, teach, or study this material, may you "grow in the grace and knowledge of our Lord and Savior Jesus Christ" (2 Pet. 3:18).

Reflections

OUR DAILY BREAD

Delivered right to your home!

You can make *Our Daily Bread* part of your regular time with God. Every month, you can receive a new booklet of devotional articles. Each day's topic is timely and lively and filled with wisdom and reliable instruction from God's Word.

To receive *Our Daily Bread* each month at home, just write to us at the address below or visit us at **www.odb.org/guide** to order online.

As part of the *Our Daily Bread* family, you'll also get opportunities to receive Bible-study guides and booklets on a variety of topics including creation, the church, and how to live the Christian life.

For program listings and other information about RBC resources, write to RBC Ministries at:

USA: PO Box 2222, Grand Rapids, MI 49501-2222
CANADA: Box 1622, Windsor, ON N9A 6Z7
RBC Web site: www.rbc.net

Support for RBC Ministries comes from the gifts of our members and friends. We are not funded or endowed by any group or denomination.